Yummy Cookie D

Safe to Taste before It Goes into the Oven

BY

Rachael Rayner

License Notes

No part of this Book can be reproduced in any form or by any means including print, electronic, scanning or photocopying unless prior permission is granted by the author.

All ideas, suggestions and guidelines mentioned here are written for informative purposes. While the author has taken every possible step to ensure accuracy, all readers are advised to follow information at their own risk. The author cannot be held responsible for personal and/or commercial damages in case of misinterpreting and misunderstanding any part of this Book

Table of Contents

Introductions

It feels like nostalgia! Cookie dough has now become the dessert that craving for memories of tasting Cookies dough while making them in your childhood. Surprisingly, people's interest in edible cookie dough is increasing, and, at the moment, edible cookie dough has become one of the hottest crazes of that stand-alone dessert.

What actually is cookie dough?

Cookie dough refers to assorted cookie ingredients that have been mixed into the malleable dough. Usually, the cookie dough will be shaped into small forms, laid on cookie sheets, and baked in the oven at a certain temperature. As a result, crispy or chewy cookies will be served on your table to accompany your special moments.

Basically, cookie dough is made from butter, sugar, eggs, and flour. However, as people become more creative, some other additional ingredients, such as milk, flavors, food colorings, chocolate, cheese, sprinkles, raisin, and many more, are often included in the cookie dough. This will generate a lot more variations of cookies that will surely tempt whoever has offered them.

One of the best parts of making cookie dough is that it is usually followed by baking is licking the cookie dough a bit or more. It is normal for, like what was mentioned before, cookie dough spreads a tempting aroma and tastes great even if it has not been heated in the oven yet.

The question now is: is it safe to eat the cookie dough raw? In the next chapters of this book, I will explain how safe cookie dough should be prepared, how to store, and other information that you should know regarding edible cookie dough.

Keep reading and stay healthy, good people!

Safe Edible Cookie Dough: Knowing the Basic

You may think that eating raw cookie dough from the mixing bowl is safe. You probably will say that you have eaten the raw cookie dough for many years of baking and have never gotten sick (knock on wood). It is true that you may not get any significant health problems. However, eating raw cookie dough puts your body at the risk of ill health.

Two ingredients that potentially cause sickness by eating raw cookie dough are raw flour and eggs. It is the Salmonella contained in raw eggs that often causes problems while eating uncooked cookie dough. It may cause fever, diarrhea, and abdominal cramping. However, Salmonella is not the only issue because E. Coli bacteria in raw flour may lead to the same symptoms. Besides, the E. Coli bacteria also cause loss of appetite, fever, and abdominal gases. Eating raw cookie dough is not the best option, and you should think twice before doing it. So now, is there any solution for this problem?

Yes, of course. The simplest way to prevent the Salmonella content in cookie dough is by making eggless cookie dough. However, if you want to involve the richness that the eggs can bring, using pasteurized eggs is the best option. With the correct technique, they are safe to eat raw. For the flour, you can toast it, so that the E. Coli bacteria disappears and then you can safely consume raw cookie dough.

Those are the best ways to trick several unsafe ingredients into generating safe edible cookie dough. Other ingredients used in cookie dough recipes such as sugar, butter, cheese, chocolate, jam, roasted nuts, and some others are usually safe to eat. There is nothing more to worry about because you have already known that you can eat cookie dough raw as long as you use the right ingredients.

To make everything about cookie dough clearer, let us go to the following chapters before hitting the recipes and make the delicious edible cookie dough in your lovely kitchen.

Safe Edible Cookie Dough: The Ingredients

The ingredients for edible cookie dough and bakeable cookies are almost the same. You just have to treat several particular ingredients before adding them to the cookie, involving them into an edible cookie dough.

Over the next page are several ingredients that are typically used to make edible cookie dough:

The Basic Ingredients

Butter

Butter is a popular dairy product that consists of butterfat and milk proteins. It will remain solid when refrigerated but will soften at room temperature and melted at around 90°F (30°C). Usually, the butter will be a pale-yellow color. However, it varies from nearly white to deep yellow, depends on the animal's food and genetics. Sometimes, the commercial industry manipulates the color of butter to make it more attractive.

Butter sometimes sold with added salt and also flavors, such as garlic, lemon-herb, honey, or cheese. They are simply made by mixing plain butter with additional flavors or ingredients.

As it is one of the basic ingredients of cookie dough, butter is must be included in the recipe. However, if you don't like butter, you can substitute with almond butter, coconut butter, or oil, as long as they can bind your ingredients into a malleable dough.

Sugar

It is obvious that sugar contributes to the sweetness level of your cookie dough. The more sugar you add, the sweeter it will be.

Some options of sugar you can use for your special cookie dough are granulated sugar, caster, powdered, brown, palm, and coconut sugar. Nevertheless, for specific reasons, some people like to substitute sugar with Stevia, Molasses, or other healthier sweetener alternative.

Flour

While making cookie dough, flours' purpose is to hold the ingredients together, resulting in a firm and malleable dough. The amount of flour is crucial to ensure the right consistency of the cookie dough—the more flour used in, the firmer it will be. On the other hand, the less flour used in, the recipe will result in a mushier dough.

Since raw flour is not recommended for edible cookie dough, first, you have to toast whatever flour you use before adding it to your decided recipe. The process of toasting the flour is very easy. You can spread flour on a baking tray and toast at 350°F for approximately 2 to 4 minutes. After that, remove from the oven and let it cool completely. The flour will be ready and safe to be used. If the oven is not available in your kitchen, you can microwave your flour on high until the internal temperature of the flour reaches 160°F.

Egg

Although there is only a small chance of Salmonella in raw eggs, it is better to ensure that whatever you put in your food is safe. Pasteurization is a great method to warrant that the eggs are safe, even if they are uncooked. Pasteurized eggs can be found in the nearest supermarket. However, the price is usually quite high. Because of that reason, why don't you pasteurize your eggs at home as it is very easy to do?

To pasteurize eggs, you have to start with fresh eggs. As a general rule, fresh eggs are better than the old ones. You can place the eggs in a pan then pour water to cover it. The eggs should be covered by approximately 1-inch water. Heat the water on the medium heat until it has reached 140°F. Use an instant-read thermometer, keep the temperature at 140°F for 3 to 5 minutes and then remove from heat. After that, remove the eggs from the hot water then rinse them with cold water. The eggs are now safe to use.

The Additional Ingredients

The additional ingredients may vary depending on how creative you are feeling. The functions of them are to enhance the aroma, give flavor, and upgrade the appearance. Here are some options that you may add to your cookie dough.

Dried fruits

Raisins, dates, prunes, figs, apricots, mangoes, pineapples, cranberries, blueberries, bananas, apples

Chocolate

Dark chocolate, chocolate chips, cocoa powder, liquid chocolate

Cheese

Cheddar cheese, cream cheese

Herbs

Basil, mint, rosemary, oregano, thyme, cilantro, parsley, chives, dill, tarragon

Spices

Ginger, cinnamon, cloves, almond extract, pumpkin spice, vanilla extract, etc.

Nuts

Roasted peanuts, roasted cashews, roasted walnuts, roasted pecans

Milk

Fresh milk, powdered milk

Coffee

Brewed coffee, cappuccino

Others

Oatmeal, honey, maple syrup, lemon zest, lime zest

Safe Edible Cookie Dough: The Basic Tools

To make cookie dough, of course, you will need several basic tools. Below is the list of tools that you may use during the cookie dough making process. However, I suggest you start with the most basic tools—start from number one and maximize whatever tools you have already had in your kitchen. Don't worry; even professional chefs started their first cooking experiences with limited equipment.

Measuring spoons

Measuring cups

A mixing bowl

Wooden or rubber spatulas

A pastry blender

Cookie scoops

A hand mixer

A food processor

A food scale

Baking tray

Safe Edible Cookie Dough: The Methods

Now, you have already understood how the safe edible cookie dough should be made, what the best ingredients are to use, and what basic tools you will need. The next step will be the making process, the storage, and the serving. In the next paragraph, I will explain the best way of each process so that you can practice the recipes in this book without any difficulty.

How To Make Safe Edible Cookie Dough

Making cookie dough is very easy. It is as simple as mixing all the ingredients in a mixing bowl while using a spatula. Since cookie dough will not rise, there is no chance to fail in making cookie dough.

To summarize the edible cookie dough making process, you can start by mixing softened butter with sugar and whatever flavorings you have chosen. If you want to use pasteurized eggs, you can put them in this process. After that, you can stir the flour into the mixture and end with additional ingredients like chocolate chips, dried fruits, nuts, etc.

However, if you like to melt the butter, you can mix all the liquid together, including milk, honey, syrup, and other liquid ingredients in a bowl. In another bowl, you can combine all the dry ingredients and stir well. Once each mixture is though roughly mixed, combine the liquid and dry mixtures and stir well or until it becomes a malleable dough.

How to Store

Once the edible cookie dough is done, you can directly eat it, bake it, or store it for later usage. As edible cookie dough is mainly made from raw ingredients, so storing it in the refrigerator is a must. Though it must be stressed that although you can store it in the fridge, it must be used within a short time. Covering with plastic wrap or aluminum foil will prevent the dough from drying out. Besides that, it should keep the tempting aroma and delicious. It can be stored in the refrigerator for 2 days.

For longer shelf life, we suggest freezing the edible cookie dough. The storage method is the same as the storage method in the refrigerator. The edible cookie dough should be wrapped and covered tightly with aluminum foil or plastic wrap.

How to Serve

The way people serve edible cookie dough may vary from one to another. It all depends on people's creativity. Basically, edible cookie dough is served just the way it is. However, to enhance the appearance and taste, you can add ice cream, fresh fruits, jam, chocolate topping, and many other garnishes, as you desired.

Due to its popularity, cookie dough is now a common dessert in my family's dining table. It has the texture of ice cream and serves the same nutrients as other sweet treats, like cakes or hot desserts. Moreover, its simple cooking process will make moms or anyone in charge in the kitchen has nothing to prepare. In conclusion, this edible dough can be a perfect dish to make and serve. You can eat the dough today and keep the rest to bake the following day.

Edible Chocolate Cookie Dough

Chocolate Brownie Cookie Dough

It is obvious that brownies are a satisfying food, no matter your age. The chocolate taste in this cookie dough brownie is so fantastic! Kids and adults alike will find it hard to ignore the taste sensation that this brownie recipe will offer.

Serving Size: 4

Cooking Time: 15 Minutes

Ingredients:

- ¾ cup butter
- ¾ cup granulated sugar
- ½ cup brown sugar
- ¼ cup cocoa powder
- 3 tablespoons olive oil
- 2 tablespoons milk powder
- 1 cup toasted flour
- ¼ teaspoon salt
- ¼ cup dark chocolate
- 1 cup chocolate chips
- 3 tablespoons colorful chocolate sprinkles

Instructions:

1. Mix toasted flour with salt, cocoa powder, and milk powder in a bowl then stir well.

2. Place butter in another bowl then add granulated sugar and brown sugar to the bowl. Using a hand mixer beat until creamy and fluffy.

3. Pour olive oil into the mixture then mix well.

4. Next, add the dry mixture to the creamy mixture then using a wooden or rubber spatula mix until combined and becoming soft dough.

5. Scoop the dough and divide into 4 cups.

6. After that, melt the dark chocolate then drizzle over the cookie dough.

7. Top the cookie dough with chocolate chips and colorful sprinkles then serve.

8. Enjoy!

Simple Chocolate Cookie Dough with Milky Chocolate Chips

Milk chocolate chip is very special. It is not too sweet and not too bitter. The additional milky taste in the milk chocolate chips is also a plus. Mixing the milk chocolate chips into cookie dough is not only the right choice but also a classic. One thing you should pay attention to is, always use high-quality milk chocolate chips.

Serving Size: 4

Cooking Time: 15 Minutes

Ingredients:

- ¾ cup butter
- ¾ cup brown sugar
- 2-½ teaspoons vanilla
- ¼ teaspoon salt
- ¾ cup toasted flour
- 2 tablespoons chocolate condensed milk
- 1 ½ cup milk chocolate chips

Instructions:

1. Place butter and sugar in a mixing bowl then using a hand mixer, mix until soft and creamy.

2. Next, add vanilla, salt, and chocolate milk to the mixture then beat until combined.

3. After that, stir toasted flour into the mixture and beat until becoming soft dough. If it is difficult to mix the flour using a hand mixer, you can mix them using a rubber or wooden spatula.

4. Remove the hand mixer from the dough then add milk chocolate chips to the dough.

5. Using a rubber or wooden spatula, mix the chocolate chips with the dough until just combined then divide the cookie dough into 4 cups.

6. Serve and enjoy.

Chocolate Blanket Cookie Dough Balls

If there is someone who doesn't like chocolate, please raise your hand. We will show you that chocolates are too good to be ignored. This cookie dough recipe uses special mini chocolate chips that are covered with melted dark chocolate. You just have to try a bite to know that you will never be able to resist!!

Serving Size: 4

Cooking Time: 1 Hour 25 Minutes

Ingredients:

- ¾ cup butter
- ½ cup brown sugar
- 2 tablespoons applesauce
- ½ teaspoon vanilla
- 1-½ cups toasted flour
- ¼ teaspoon salt
- ¾ cup mini chocolate chips
- 1-cup dark chocolate
- 2 tablespoons milk

Instructions:

1. Place butter in a mixing bowl together with brown sugar, applesauce, and vanilla then using a hand mixer beat until creamy.

2. Stir in toasted flour and salt to the mixture then using a wooden spatula mix until combined.

3. Next, add mini chocolate chips to the dough then stir well.

4. Scoop the cookie dough and shape into small balls forms then arrange on a baking tray.

5. Freeze the balls for at least 30 minutes or until firm.

6. In the meantime, melt dark chocolate in a microwave then pour milk over the melted chocolate. Stir until incorporated.

7. After 30 minutes, remove the cookie dough balls from the freezer.

8. Take a cookie ball then dip in the melted chocolate and make sure the cookie ball is completely coated with melted chocolate. Repeat with the remaining cookie balls and melted chocolate.

9. Arrange the coated cookie dough balls on a baking tray then refrigerate for another 30 minutes or until set.

10. Remove the coated cookie dough balls from the refrigerator and serve.

11. Enjoy!

Chocolate Matcha Cookie Dough with Sweet Date

You will never know that matcha and chocolate serve a very special taste until you try this cookie dough. The dates used in this recipe also give a natural sweetness that is not only tasty but also healthier. The appearance of these cookie dough balls may be pale. To enhance the appearance, you may drizzle melted colorful chocolate over cookie dough balls and top with chocolate sprinkles.

Serving Size: 4

Cooking Time: 45 Minutes

Ingredients:

- ½ cup toasted flour
- 2 tablespoons cocoa powder
- 3 cups pitted dates
- ¼ cup matcha powder
- ¼ teaspoon salt
- 3 tablespoons chocolate condensed milk
- ¼ cup mini chocolate chips

Instructions:

1. Place toasted flour, cocoa powder, pitted dates, matcha powder, and salt in a food processor.

2. Drizzle chocolate condensed milk over the ingredients then process them until combined.

3. Transfer the mixture to a bowl then add mini chocolate chips to the mixture. Mix well.

4. Shape the dough into small balls forms then arrange on a baking tray.

5. Refrigerate the cookie dough balls for at least 30 minutes or until set.

6. Serve and enjoy cold.

Chocolate Cookie Dough Simple Praline

Take this praline cookie dough and put it in your mouth! The chocolate will be melting inside your mouth before you know it and soon after, you will be surprised by the nutty tasting cookie dough that will make you crave for more. This chocolate cookie dough praline is not only delicious for an everyday snack or dessert but is also perfect to be served for special occasions.

Serving Size: 4

Cooking Time: 45 Minutes

Ingredients:

- ¾ cup brown sugar
- ½ cup butter
- 2 tablespoons fresh milk
- 1-cup toasted flour
- ¼ teaspoon salt
- 1 cup chopped dark chocolate
- 1-teaspoon vegetable oil
- ½ cup mini chocolate chips

Instructions:

1. Place butter and brown sugar in a mixing bowl then using a mixer beat until creamy.

2. Add fresh milk to the butter mixture then beat again for a few seconds until incorporated. Remove the mixer.

3. After that, stir in toasted flour and salt to the mixture.

4. Using a rubber or wooden spatula stir the ingredients until becoming soft dough. Set aside.

5. Next, melt chopped dark chocolate over low heat then mix with the vegetable oil.

6. Brush melted chocolate in lots of candy molds then refrigerate for about 10 minutes or until the chocolate is set.

7. Fill each candy mold with cookie dough then cover with melted chocolate on top.

8. Return the filled chocolate to the refrigerator then refrigerate for another 10 minutes or until set. You can also put them in the freezer.

9. Unmold the filled chocolate then enjoy cold.

Super Rich Chocolate Cookie Dough

Who can refuse the delicacy of chocolate, especially a sweet snack with extra chocolate? We cannot agree more that this cookie dough is the richest one. If you like the nutty taste, you may add any kind of roasted nuts to this dough. Almonds, pecans, walnuts, and cashews are always the best choices for this cookie dough. Not to mention, dried fruits.

Serving Size: 4

Cooking Time: 45 Minutes

Ingredients:

- 1 cup toasted flour
- 3 tablespoons toasted coconut flour
- 2 tablespoons cocoa powder
- 2 tablespoons chocolate milk powder
- ¼ teaspoon salt
- ½ cup Nutella
- 2 tablespoons granulated sugar
- 3 tablespoons maple syrup
- 2 tablespoons chocolate condensed milk
- 3 tablespoons chopped roasted hazelnuts
- 3 tablespoons mini chocolate chips

Instructions:

1. Place the dry mixture—toasted flour, coconut flour, cocoa powder, chocolate milk powder, salt, and granulated sugar in a bowl then stir until combined.

2. Add Nutella to the dry mixture then mix until becoming crumbles.

3. Next, drizzle maple syrup and chocolate condensed milk over the crumbles then mix until becoming soft cookie dough.

4. After that, stir in chopped roasted hazelnuts and mini chocolate chips to the dough then mix well.

5. Shape the cookie dough into small balls forms then arrange on a baking tray.

6. Refrigerate the cookie dough balls for at least 30 minutes or until firm then remove from the refrigerator.

7. Arrange the cookie dough balls on a serving dish then serve.

8. Enjoy cold!

Triple Chocolate Cookie Dough

What will happen if dark chocolate is combined with cocoa powder and chocolate protein powder? This book is proudly presenting this triple chocolate cookie dough recipe. Not only does it have a delicious chocolate taste, but this cookie dough also offers special nutrition from protein powder. Serve this for breakfast and get enough energy to last you through the day.

Serving Size: 4

Cooking Time: 20 Minutes

Ingredients:

- 1-cup chocolate protein powder
- ¼ cup toasted flour
- 3 tablespoons cocoa powder
- ¼ cup brown sugar
- ½ cup butter
- ¼ cup chopped dark chocolate
- ¼ cup coconut flakes

Instructions:

1. Melt butter over very low heat together with chopped dark chocolate then set aside.

2. Combine the dry ingredients—chocolate protein powder, toasted flour, cocoa powder, and brown sugar in a bowl then stir well.

3. Pour the melted butter and chocolate over the dry mixture then using a rubber or wooden spatula mix until becoming soft dough.

4. Take a scoop of cookie dough then shape into small balls form. Repeat with the remaining dough.

5. Arrange the cookie dough balls on a serving dish then sprinkle coconut flakes on top.

6. Serve and enjoy.

Chocolate Brownies Cookie Dough Layers

If you are looking for a nutritious but practical lunch, this cookie dough may be the answer. It is a collaboration between delicious brownies, soft cookie dough, and melted chocolate. For sure, the nutritious content in this cookie dough is beneficial. Besides that, the appearance is surprisingly beautiful. Serve this cookie dough with black coffee while entertaining your guests seems to be a great option.

Serving Size: 4

Cooking Time: 30 Minutes

Ingredients:

- ½ cup almond butter
- ¼ cup granulated sugar
- ½ cup brown sugar
- 2 tablespoons fresh milk
- 1-teaspoon vanilla
- ¾ cup toasted flour
- ¼ teaspoon salt
- ¼ cup mini chocolate chips
- 1-layer brownies
- ¼ cup chopped dark chocolate
- 2 tablespoons butter

Instructions:

1. Place almond butter, brown sugar, and granulated sugar in a mixing bowl then using a mixer beat until creamy.

2. Add fresh milk and vanilla to the mixture then beat again until incorporated. Remove the mixer.

3. Next, add toasted flour and salt to the mixture then using a wooden or rubber spatula mix until becoming soft dough.

4. Stir in mini chocolate chips to the soft dough then mix well.

5. Line a baking pan with parchment paper then place brownies in it.

6. Top the brownies with cookie dough then spread evenly. Refrigerate for 10 minutes.

7. In the meantime, melt chopped dark chocolate over medium heat then add butter to the chocolate. Stir until incorporated and let it cool.

8. After 10 minutes in the refrigerator, take the cookie dough out of the refrigerator then brush chocolate and butter mixture on top.

9. Return to the refrigerator for approximately 5 minutes then cut into small squares.

10. Serve and enjoy.

Edible Fruit Cookie Dough

Cinnamon Honey Pumpkin Cookie Dough

There is no doubt that pumpkin is a nutritious squash that is rich in essential minerals and vitamins. Including pumpkin in cookie dough does not only make it delicious but also beneficial for your health, leaving you feeling re-energized.

Serving Size: 4

Cooking Time: 15 Minutes

Ingredients:

- ½ cup pumpkin puree
- ½ cup butter
- ¼ cup raw honey
- 1 tablespoon pumpkin spice
- 1 ½ teaspoons cinnamon
- 1 cup toasted flour
- ½ cup diced dark chocolate

Instructions:

1. Place butter and pumpkin puree in a mixing bowl then using an electric mixer whisk until incorporated.

2. Drizzle raw honey over the butter mixture then add pumpkin spice and cinnamon.

3. Continue whisking until the batter is smooth and incorporated. Remove the electric mixer then set aside.

4. Next, add toasted flour to the mixture then using a wooden spatula stir the mixture until becoming soft dough.

5. After that, stir in diced dark chocolate then mix well.

6. Divide the dough into several cups then tightly cover with the lid.

7. Refrigerate the cookie dough for at least 3 hours then enjoy as a snack or dessert.

Strawberry Milky Ice Cream Cookie Dough

An ice cream may be a perfect choice for cooling down on a hot day. This strawberry cookie dough is safe and nutritious as ice cream. With fresh strawberries and heavy cream, this ice cream cookie offers refreshing energy and ice delicious flavor all at the same time. To enrich the strawberry taste, you can also add fresh chopped strawberries to the cookie dough. You can also use the frozen strawberries if you want to save time.

Serving Size: 4

Cooking Time: 4 Hours 15 Minutes

Ingredients:

- 1-cup fresh strawberries
- ½ cup whole milk
- ¼ cup granulated sugar
- ¼ teaspoon salt
- 1-cup heavy cream
- 1-teaspoon vanilla

Instructions:

1. Place strawberries in a food processor then process until smooth. Set aside.

2. Pour milk in a bowl then add sugar and salt to the bowl. Stir until the salt and sugar are dissolved.

3. Next, stir in heavy cream, vanilla, and strawberry puree then mix until incorporated.

4. Move the mixture to an ice cream maker then follow the machine directions.

5. Once it is done, scoop the strawberry ice cream cookie dough and drop on a cone.

6. Serve and enjoy cold.

Banana Butter Cookie Dough

Are you a big fan of bananas? If so, you must be very interested in this cookie dough. It is very simple and easy to prepare. It is also a great option for breakfast since the banana contains lots of carbohydrates and vitamins, which are very good for your body. The key of this cookie dough is by using ripe or overripe bananas. You should never use half-ripe bananas as they are not sweet enough. Also, half-ripe bananas will be more difficult to mash.

Serving Size: 4

Cooking Time: 15 Minutes

Ingredients:

- 4 ripe bananas
- ¼ cup vanilla protein powder
- ¼ cup granulated sugar
- ½ cup toasted coconut flour
- ½ cup butter
- ¼ cup honey
- 3 tablespoons milk
- ¼ cup chocolate chips

Instructions:

1. Melt butter over medium heat then combine with honey. Stir until incorporated then set aside.

2. Next, peel and cut the bananas into thick slices then place in a bowl.

3. Using a spoon or any tools you have mash the bananas until smooth and creamy.

4. After that, add granulated sugar, vanilla protein powder, and toasted coconut flour to the mashed banana. Mix well.

5. Drizzle melted butter and milk over the banana mixture then stir until combined and becoming soft dough.

6. Divide the banana cookie dough into 4 cups then sprinkle chocolate chips on top.

7. Serve and enjoy.

Blueberry Oatmeal Cookie Dough

Oatmeal is famous for its delicious taste and high nutritional content. Including oatmeal in cookie dough will surely give lots of health benefits, including lowering your cholesterol levels, protecting heart health, and controlling weight. Combining this oatmeal cookie dough with blueberry is also a smart idea since blueberry is a great source of antioxidant. You can add other berries such as blackberries, cranberries, or raspberries.

Serving Size: 4

Cooking Time: 15 Minutes

Ingredients:

- ¾ cup butter
- ¾ cup brown sugar
- ¼ cup granulated sugar
- 2 pasteurized eggs
- 1 ½ teaspoons vanilla
- 2 cups quick cooking oats
- 2 cups blueberries

Instructions:

1. Place butter, vanilla, and brown sugar in a mixing bowl then using a mixer beat until smooth and creamy.

2. Crack the pasteurized eggs then add to the mixing bowl. Beat again until fluffy then remove the mixer.

3. Cut the blueberries into halves then add to the mixture together with quick cooking oats and granulated sugar.

4. Using a wooden or rubber spatula mix the ingredients until becoming soft dough then divide into 4 cups.

5. Serve and enjoy.

Lemon Lime Cookie Dough

As a great source of vitamin C, both lemon and lime do not only offer anti-wrinkles benefits but also a refreshing taste and aroma. Once you scoop out this cookie dough, you will quickly be tempted with its aroma, and once it touches your tongue, you will definitely be surprised by its mouthwatering taste. If you like a citrusy taste, you can add the lime and lemon juice. However, I do not recommend you add the grated zest because If you use it too much, the cookie dough will end up tasting bitter.

Serving Size: 4

Cooking Time: 30 Minutes

Ingredients:

- ¾ cup butter
- ¾ cup coconut sugar
- ¼ teaspoon salt
- 3 tablespoons lemon juice
- A pinch grated lemon zest
- 1-¼ cups toasted flour
- 2 fresh limes

Instructions:

1. Place butter and coconut sugar in a mixing bowl then using a mixer beat until smooth and creamy.

2. Add salt and grated lemon zest to the mixture then pour lemon juice over the creamy butter. Beat until fluffy.

3. Next, add toasted flour to the mixture and using a wooden or rubber spatula mix until becoming soft dough.

4. Cover the cookie dough with plastic wrap then refrigerate for about 15 minutes.

5. After 15 minutes, remove the cookie dough from the refrigerator and divide into 4 cups.

6. Cut the limes into halves then drizzle the juice over the cookie dough.

7. Serve and enjoy.

Refreshing Orange Cookie Dough with Caramel Sauce

Are you looking for a citrusy cookie dough recipe? If yes, then you should try this cookie dough. While other cookie dough offers chocolate or milky flavors, this recipe serves as a citrusy and sweet cookie dough. It is a great option when you want to taste something sweet but light.

Serving Size: 4

Cooking Time: 20 Minutes

Ingredients:

- ¾ cup butter
- ¾ cup powdered sugar
- ¼ teaspoon salt
- 1-¼ cups toasted almond flour
- ¼ cup orange juice
- ½ teaspoon grated orange juice
- ¼ cup water
- ¾ cup granulated sugar
- ¼ teaspoon vanilla
- ¼ cup heavy cream

Instructions:

1. Place granulated sugar in a saucepan then heat over very low heat.

2. Once the sugar is melted, pour water over the sugar and stir until dissolved.

3. Stir in vanilla and heavy cream to the mixture then bring to a simmer.

4. Remove the caramel sauce from heat and let it cool and thicken. Set aside.

5. Place butter and powdered sugar in a mixing bowl then using a mixer beat until creamy.

6. Add salt, grated lemon juice, and orange juice to the mixing bowl then stir until combined.

7. Next, add toasted almond flour to the mixture and using a rubber or wooden spatula mix until becoming soft dough.

8. Divide the cookie dough into 4 cups then drizzle caramel sauce on top.

9. Serve and enjoy.

Oatmeal Raisins Cookie Dough with Rum

There is no doubt that oatmeal is a beneficial ingredient that also serves a delicious taste. However, raisins and rum in this oatmeal cookie dough surely what makes it special. Raisins are often sold in dried forms. To enjoy them, it is suggested to soak the raisins in boiling water for 10 minutes before straining and using them in your cooking. The raisins will be softer, juicer, and plumper.

Serving Size: 4

Cooking Time: 20 Minutes

Ingredients:

- ¾ cup butter
- ¾ cup palm sugar
- ¾ teaspoon vanilla
- ¼ cup fresh milk
- ¾ teaspoons cinnamon
- 1-cup quick cooking oats
- ¼ cup toasted almond flour
- ¾ cup raisins
- ½ cup chopped roasted walnuts
- 2 tablespoons rum

Instructions:

1. Place butter in a mixing bowl then add palm sugar in it.

2. Using a mixer beat the butter and palm sugar until becoming a creamy mixture then stir in vanilla and rum to the mixture. Mix well.

3. Pour fresh milk over the mixture then add toasted flour and quick cooking oats to the mixture. Using a wooden and rubber spatula mix until becoming soft dough.

4. Add raisins and chopped roasted walnuts to the dough then mix until just combined.

5. Divide the dough into 4 cups then serve.

6. Enjoy!

Avocado Choco Cookie Dough with Shredded Coconut

Avocado and chocolate will absolutely make your mind blow. This avocado and chocolate cookie dough is very tasty and silky. With the additional shredded coconut, there is no doubt that this dough tastes wonderful. Not only will adults like it, but children will also be big fans. Add more chopped chocolate if you like and also drizzle chocolate sauce on top to enhance the taste.

Serving Size: 4

Cooking Time: 20 Minutes

Ingredients:

- ¾ cup butter
- 1-cup quick cooking oats
- ¼ cup toasted flour
- 3 tablespoons cocoa powder
- 1-cup brown sugar
- 2 ripe avocados
- ½ cup shredded coconuts
- ½ cup chopped dark chocolate

Instructions:

1. Cut the avocados into halves then discard the seeds.

2. Scoop out the avocado flesh then place in a bowl. Mash until smooth.

3. Add brown sugar and cocoa powder to the mashed avocado then mix until the mashed avocados turn into brown.

4. Next, stir in toasted flour to the mashed avocado then mix until creamy.

5. After that, add quick cooking oats, granulated sugar, and shredded coconut to the mixture then mix well.

6. Divide the cookie dough into 4 cups and sprinkle chopped dark chocolate on top.

7. Serve and enjoy.

Cheesy Confetti Cookie Dough

This dough will remind you of the colorful confetti and candies that pop out of a pinata after you've hit it hard. It is the rainbow sprinkle that adds the colors in your pale dough. The sprinkles also give crunchy texture when you chew the cheesy dough. The light sweet taste is a great combination with the cheese flavor.

Serving Size: 4

Cooking Time: 3 Hours 15 Minutes

Ingredients:

- ½ cup butter
- ½ cup cream cheese
- ½ cup brown sugar
- ½ teaspoon vanilla
- ¾ cup mini chocolate chips
- ½ cup rainbow sprinkles
- ½ cup silver sprinkles

Instructions:

1. Place butter and cream cheese in a mixing bowl then beat using a hand mixer until creamy.

2. Add vanilla and brown sugar to the mixture then beat again until combined.

3. Next, stir in mini chocolate chips to the mixture and mix well.

4. After that, prepare a sheet of plastic wrap on a flat surface then place the cookie dough on it.

5. Shape the cookie dough into a big ball then wrap with the plastic wrap.

6. Refrigerate the cookie dough ball for 3 hours. It is better if you shape the semi-firm ball once again after 2 hours.

7. In the meantime, place the rainbow sprinkles and silver sprinkles in a bowl then mix well.

8. After 3 hours, remove the ball from the refrigerator then discard the plastic wrap.

9. If the ball is firm enough, you can roll it into the sprinkle mixture. However, if it is not, simply sprinkle the rainbow and silver sprinkles over the ball.

10. Serve and enjoy.

Cream Cheese Cookie Dough with Vanilla Ice Cream

Combining cream cheese cookie dough with vanilla ice cream is like mixing two kinds of happiness in one small cup. Both have a delicate texture and taste that will make you feel difficult to stop once you take your first spoon. It should be served while the dough is cold.

Serving Size: 4

Cooking Time: 55 Minutes

Ingredients:

- ½ cup almond butter
- ½ cup cream cheese
- ¼ cup brown sugar
- 1-½ cups toasted flour
- 4 scoops vanilla ice cream

Instructions:

1. Place almond butter and cream cheese in a mixing bowl then using a mixer beat until creamy.

2. Add brown sugar to the cream cheese mixture then beat again until combined. Remove the mixer.

3. Next, add toasted flour to the cream cheese mixture then mix until becoming dough.

4. Cover the dough with plastic wrap then refrigerate for 15 minutes.

5. After 15 minutes, take the dough out of the refrigerator then shape the dough into very small balls. Each ball will be around ½ teaspoon.

6. Arrange the cookie dough small balls on a baking tray then refrigerate again for another 15 minutes.

7. Place a scoop of vanilla ice cream in a cup then arrange cookie dough balls on top.

8. Serve and enjoy.

Vanilla Cheesy Cookie Dough Ball with Pecan Coating

Don't just serve it in chunks or scoops. You can roll it in balls shape then put it on the chopped pecan so that the dough will be coated with the crunchy nuts. The taste is so rich, for it mixes the sweetness and creamy vanilla taste with the salty, cheesy flavor. It can be used as a snack for your lunch bag.

Serving Size: 4

Cooking Time: 4 Hours 15 Minutes

Ingredients:

- ¾ cup cream cheese
- ¾ cup butter
- 1-teaspoon vanilla
- ¾ cup powdered sugar
- ¼ cup brown sugar
- 1 ½ cup mini chocolate chips
- 1-½ cups chopped roasted pecans

Instructions:

1. Using a mixer soften cream cheese in a mixing bowl then add vanilla and butter to the bowl.

2. Beat those ingredients until creamy then stir in powdered sugar and granulated sugar. Mix well.

3. Next, add mini chocolate chips to the mixture then mix until just combined.

4. Transfer the mixture to a sheet of plastic wrap then wrap the mixture and bind it tightly on top.

5. Freeze for approximately 10 to 15 minutes and shape into a big ball.

6. Return the ball to the freezer and freeze for an hour more. Reshape the ball once every 10 minutes to make it perfect.

7. Once the cheese cookie dough ball is firm, remove from the freezer and unwrap it.

8. Roll the cheese cookie dough ball in the chopped roasted pecans then serve.

9. Enjoy immediately.

Rich Cheese Cookie Dough with Brownie

If chocolate and cheese are your favorite flavors, you can combine both of them in this delicious dessert. One great tip is to make the cheese dough much cheesier and the chocolate brownie sweet. The combination will make your taste buds happy.

Serving Size: 4

Cooking Time: 40 Minutes

Ingredients:

- ½ cup peanut butter
- ½ cup brown sugar
- 2 cups cream cheese
- 1-teaspoon vanilla
- ¼ teaspoon salt
- 1 cup toasted flour
- ¼ cup grated cheddar cheese
- ¼ cup butter
- ½ cup heavy cream
- 2 layers brownies

Instructions:

1. Place butter in a mixer then beat until soft.

2. Add 1 ½ cups cream cheese together with heavy cream to the butter then mix well. Set aside.

3. Next, place peanut butter, brown sugar, and ½ cup cream cheese in a mixing bowl then using a mixer beat until creamy.

4. Add salt and vanilla to the mixture then beat for a few seconds until incorporated. Remove the mixer.

5. Stir in cheddar cheese and toasted flour to the mixture then using a wooden or rubber spatula mix until becoming soft dough.

6. Prepare a baking pan and layer with parchment paper.

7. Place a layer of brownie in it then cover with half of the heavy cream and cream cheese mixture.

8. Spread the cookie dough over the brownies then cover the cookie dough with the remaining heavy cream mixture.

9. Top the layers with another brownie then refrigerate for approximately 20 minutes.

10. Cut into wedges then arrange on a serving dish.

11. Serve and enjoy.

Cookie Dough Cheesy Sandwich

If you want a different way of serving cookie dough, this sandwich is a great option. It is best to be served at a small party or packed in a sealed container for an outing gathering or a picnic. Cut in a small, one bite rectangular or triangle shape to make it more appealing.

Serving Size: 4

Cooking Time: 4 Hours 20 Minutes

Ingredients:

- ¾ cup butter
- ¾ cup grated Cheddar cheese
- 3 tablespoons fresh milk
- 1-½ cups toasted flour
- ½ cup mini chocolate chips
- 2 cups whipped cream
- 1-cup cream cheese

Instructions:

1. Prepare 2 baking pan then line each pan with parchment paper. Set aside.

2. Place butter and grated Cheddar cheese in a mixing bowl then using a mixer beat until creamy.

3. Pour fresh milk into the mixture then beat again until incorporated. Remove the mixer.

4. Add toasted flour to the mixture then using a rubber or wooden spatula mix until becoming soft dough.

5. After that, stir in mini chocolate chips to the dough then mix well.

6. Divide the soft dough into 2 then press each part into the prepared pan then freeze for an hour.

7. In the meantime, place cream cheese in a mixing bowl then beat until soft.

8. Pour whipped cream over the cream cheese then beat on high speed until creamy.

9. Refrigerate the cream cheese mixture until set.

10. To serve, take a part of cookie dough then place on a flat surface.

11. Cover the cookie dough with cream cheese and the whipped cream mixture then top with another cookie dough layer.

12. Refrigerate the cookie dough sandwich for at least 3 hours then cut into small squares.

13. Arrange on a serving dish then serve.

14. Enjoy!

Spicy Cheese Cookie Dough Balls Jalapeno

Who says that cookie recipes must always be sweet? You might get a surprise that jalapeno is a good match for cheese. They can even be the main ingredients of your cookie dough. This recipe can also function as a dip to your chips or fried potatoes. You can even use it to spread on your toast or have in a sandwich.

Serving Size: 4

Cooking Time: 1 Hour 20 Minutes

Ingredients:

- 2 cups grated cheddar cheese
- ½ cup softened cream cheese
- ¾ tablespoon onion powder
- ¾ tablespoon garlic powder
- 10 jalapenos
- ¼ cup diced bacon

Instructions:

1. Remove the jalapeno seeds then cut the jalapenos into very small dices.

2. Combine the entire ingredients—grated cheddar cheese, softened cream cheese, onion powder, garlic powder, diced jalapenos, and diced bacon in a bowl then mix well.

3. Transfer the cheese mixture to a sheet of plastic wrap or aluminum foil then wrap the whole mixture tightly and shape into a bog ball.

4. Refrigerate the cheese ball for at least 2 hours and re-shape once every 15 minutes.

5. Once the cheese cookie dough ball is firm, remove from the refrigerator and serve with crackers.

6. Enjoy!

Edible Nutty Cookie Dough

Sweet and Soft Peanut Cookie Dough

This peanut cookie dough is very easy and simple to prepare. It presents a nutty taste that will satisfy every peanut lover in this world. You can always enjoy this cookie dough simply just the way it is. However, if you want more variations, you can add chocolate chips, sprinkles, and other toppings you desire.

Serving Size: 4

Cooking Time: 15 Minutes

Ingredients:

- ½ cup peanut butter
- ¼ cup peanut jam
- ½ cup brown sugar
- ¼ teaspoon salt
- ¾ cup toasted flour
- 3 tablespoons milk

Instructions:

1. Place peanut butter and peanut jam in a mixing bowl then beat until soft.

2. Add brown sugar to the mixture and beat again with the hand mixer until creamy.

3. Next, stir salt and toasted flour into the mixture and mix until becoming dough.

4. After that, pour milk over the dough and stir until combined.

5. Divide the dough into 4 cups then serve.

6. Enjoy!

Cold Almond Cookie Dough Balls

Hello, almond lovers! This cookie dough offers you a very nutty taste since it uses almonds in many forms, from butter, flour, to milk. For sure, this cookie dough is a representative of almonds. If you really like the almond taste, you may substitute vanilla with almond extract. Besides that, you can also add chopped roasted almonds to the cookie dough, replacing the chocolate chips or accompanying them.

Serving Size: 4

Cooking Time: 15 Minutes

Ingredients:

- ¾ cup almond butter
- ½ cup powdered sugar
- ½ cup toasted almond flour
- ½ cup toasted flour
- 1-teaspoon vanilla
- 2 tablespoons almond milk
- ¼ cup mini chocolate chips

Instructions:

1. Place almond butter, vanilla, condensed milk, and powdered sugar in a mixing bowl then beat until just combined. Remove the mixer.

2. Add toasted almond flour and toasted flour to the mixture then using a rubber or wooden spatula mix well.

3. Next, stir in the mini chocolate chips and mix until just combined.

4. Shape the cookie dough into small balls forms then place on a tray.

5. Refrigerate the almond cookie dough balls for at least an hour until firm and cold.

6. Serve and enjoy whenever you want.

Crispy Peanut Cookie Dough

Any kinds of nuts can actually be used in your cookie dough. The most popular one is chopped peanut. Great tip: you can both bake the peanuts or simply dry stir them in your wok to provide a better taste.

Serving Size: 4

Cooking Time: 20 Minutes

Ingredients:

- ¾ cup peanut butter
- ¾ cup powdered sugar
- 2 tablespoons peanut jam
- 1-teaspoon vanilla
- ¼ cup rice cereal
- ¾ cup roasted peanuts

Instructions:

1. Place the roasted peanuts in a food processor then process until becoming flour. Set aside.

2. Combine peanut butter with peanut jam and powdered sugar then using a hand mixer beat until creamy.

3. Next, pour vanilla into the creamy mixture then stir well.

4. After that, stir the roasted peanut flour and rice cereal into the mixture then mix until incorporated.

5. Shape the dough into small ball forms then arrange on a serving dish.

6. Serve and enjoy.

Dark Almond Cookie Dough

You can actually create 2 kinds of almond cookie dough from this single recipe. First is to follow the steps by grinding the almond and dates in a food processor, then mix it together with the dough. Second, you can also make the dough and put whole almonds and some tiny pieces of dates in the middle to give a nice surprise.

Serving Size: 4

Cooking Time: 20 Minutes

Ingredients:

- 2 cups roasted almonds
- ¾ cup toasted almond flour
- 1 cup pitted dates
- 1 ½ teaspoons vanilla
- ½ cup chopped dark chocolate
- 2 tablespoons cocoa powder

Instructions:

1. Melt chopped dark chocolate over medium heat then remove from heat. Let it cool.

2. Next, place roasted almonds and dates in a food processor then process until combined and smooth.

3. Transfer the almond and date mixture to a mixing bowl then add cocoa powder to the bowl. Mix well until the mixture turns to brown.

4. Add vanilla and toasted almond flour to the mixture then drizzle melted chocolate over it. Using a rubber or wooden spatula mix until becoming dark brown cookie dough.

5. Shape the cookie dough into small balls forms then place on a serving dish.

6. Serve and enjoy.

Butter-Less Cashew Cookie Dough

Do not imagine that this butter-less dough will be dry and not delicious. In fact, this dough is still soft and tasty. The secret is the cashews that will make this so mouthwatering.

Serving Size: 4

Cooking Time: 50 Minutes

Ingredients:

- 2 cups roasted cashews
- 1-cup quick cooking oats
- ¼ cup maple syrup
- 2-½ tablespoons honey
- 1 ½ tablespoons vanilla

Instructions:

1. Place the roasted cashews and quick cooking oats in a food processor then process until becoming flour.

2. Transfer the cashew and oats flour to a mixing bowl then pour maple syrup, honey, and vanilla over the flour.

3. Stir the entire ingredients until combined and becoming dough then shape into small balls forms.

4. Arrange the cookie dough balls on a baking tray then refrigerate for at least 30 minutes.

5. Once the cookie dough balls are firm, remove from the refrigerator and serve.

6. Enjoy!

Peanut Cookie Dough with Chickpeas

Peanuts are a great source of protein if I may say to myself. Peanuts and chickpeas, combined with the chocolate coating, will make this dough taste fantastic. It is best served cold, so place it in the container and store it in the fridge.

Serving Size: 4

Cooking Time: 20 Minutes

Ingredients:

- 1-½ cups canned chickpeas
- ¼ cup peanut butter
- 2 tablespoons peanut jam
- ¼ cup raw honey
- 1-½ teaspoons vanilla
- 2 teaspoons powdered sugar
- ¼ teaspoon salt
- 3 tablespoons mini chocolate chips
- 1 cup chopped dark chocolate

Instructions:

1. Place chickpeas, peanut butter, peanut jam, honey, vanilla, powdered sugar, and salt in a food processor then process until becoming soft dough.

2. Transfer the soft dough to a bowl then stir mini chocolate chips into the dough. Mix until just combined.

3. Shape the soft cookie dough into small balls forms then arrange on a baking tray.

4. Freeze the cookie dough balls in the freezer for 30 minutes or until firm.

5. In the meantime, melt the dark chocolate and let it warm.

6. After 30 minutes, take the cookie dough balls out of the freezer then dip each cookie dough ball in the melted chocolate.

7. Arrange the coated cookie dough balls on a baking tray and refrigerate for at least 15 minutes or until the chocolate is set.

8. Remove from the refrigerator and serve.

9. Enjoy!

Almond Honey Cookie Dough with Healthy Coconut Sugar

Peanuts and chickpeas, covered in a chocolate coating, will make the dough taste fantastic. Place them into a container and store it in the fridge.

Serving Size: 4

Cooking Time: 1 Hour 20 Minutes

Ingredients:

- ½ cup quick cooking oats
- 1 cup roasted almonds
- 1-¼ cups pitted dates
- 2 tablespoons coconut sugar
- 3 tablespoons almond butter
- 2 tablespoons honey
- 1-teaspoon vanilla

Instructions:

1. Place quick cooking oats in a food processor then process until becoming flour.

2. Add roasted almonds to the food processor then process again until becoming flour too.

3. Next, add pitted dates, almond butter, and coconut sugar to the food processor then drizzle honey and vanilla over the mixture. Process until combined and becoming soft cookie dough.

4. Shape the cookie dough into small balls forms then arrange on a baking tray.

5. Refrigerate the cookie dough balls for at least an hour then serve.

6. Enjoy!

Caramel Stuffed Peanut Cookie Dough

Imagine when you take one small ball and chew it. Only to find a delicious caramel center that literally melts in your mouth. It is such delicate dough that can be served to your family or guests on any occasion. This simple recipe is also a kids' favorite.

Serving Size: 4

Cooking Time: 1 Hour 20 Minutes

Ingredients:

- ¾ cup peanut butter
- ¾ cup brown sugar
- 2 pasteurized eggs
- 2 teaspoons vanilla
- ½ cup peanut jam
- 1-¼ cups roasted peanuts
- 1 cup toasted flour
- ½ cup heavy cream
- ¼ cup water
- ½ cup granulated sugar
- 1-tablespoon maple syrup
- ¼ teaspoon salt

Instructions:

1. Pour water into a pot then bring to boil.

2. Add granulated sugar to the pot then bring to a simmer until the sugar is dissolved.

3. Remove the pot from heat then stir in maple syrup and salt. Stir well and set aside.

4. In another saucepan, warm the heavy cream then pour over the sugar mixture. Stir until incorporated then let it cool.

5. Next, place the roasted peanuts in a food processor then process until becoming flour. Set aside.

6. After that, combine peanut butter with brown sugar and pasteurized eggs then beat until fluffy and creamy.

7. Add vanilla and peanut jam to the mixture then beat until incorporated. Remove the mixer.

8. Add peanut flour and toasted flour to the mixture then using a wooden or rubber spatula mix until becoming soft dough.

9. Shape the cookie dough into small balls forms and make a hole on each cookie dough ball.

10. Fill each hole with caramel sauce then arrange the cookie dough balls on a serving dish.

11. Refrigerate the cookie dough balls for an hour or until the caramel is set.

12. Serve and enjoy.

Mixed Nuts Cookie Dough with Sweet Maple

Maple syrup is one of the most commonly used syrups that is a must-buy item for every household's shopping list. The fragrant smell of its sweetness always puts a spell on everyone. When added to the dough, it will not only enhance the taste but also increase the aroma so that you and your loved ones will be eager to try it.

Serving Size: 4

Cooking Time: 15 Minutes

Ingredients:

- ¾ cup toasted almond flour
- ¼ cup ground flax
- ¼ cup roasted pecans
- ¼ cup roasted walnuts
- ¼ cup shredded coconut
- ¾ cup brown sugar
- ¼ teaspoon salt
- 2 tablespoons coconut milk
- ¼ cup maple syrup
- 1-teaspoon vanilla
- ¼ cup mini chocolate chips

Instructions:

1. Place almond flour, ground flax, roasted pecans, roasted walnuts, shredded coconut, salt, vanilla, and brown sugar in a food processor. Process until combined and becoming flour.

2. Transfer the nut mixture to a mixing bowl then drizzle coconut milk and maple syrup over it.

3. Using a wooden or rubber spatula mix the ingredients until becoming cookie dough then add mini chocolate chips to the dough. Mix until just combined.

4. Take a scoop of cookie dough then drop on a serving cup.

5. Repeat with the remaining cookie dough then serve.

6. Enjoy right away.

Sweet Coconut Almond Cookie Dough

When combined, coconut and almond can create extraordinary taste. Mix them in your cookie dough, and you will have an extremely great texture and taste. This dough must be served cold to enhance flavor.

Serving Size: 4

Cooking Time: 45 Minutes

Ingredients:

- ¾ cup almond butter
- ¾ cup pitted dates
- 1-½ cups roasted almonds
- ½ cup shredded coconut
- 2 tablespoons coconut oil
- ¼ cup mini chocolate chips

Instructions:

1. Place the roasted almonds in a food processor then process until smooth. Set aside.

2. Next, place almond butter in mixing bowl then beat until smooth and fluffy.

3. Add pitted dates to the mixing bowl then beat until incorporated.

4. After that, stir almond flour into the mixture then using a wooden or rubber spatula mix until becoming soft dough.

5. Drizzle coconut oil to the dough then add shredded coconut and mini chocolate chips to the dough. Mix well.

6. Shape the dough into small balls forms then arrange on a baking tray.

7. Refrigerate for at least 30 minutes then serve,

8. Enjoy cold!

Other Edible Cookies Dough

Sweet Brown Cookie Dough

Who doesn't love chocolate chips? The crunchy texture of the chips, combined with the softness dough, will make everyone's day. It can also transform into delicious chocolate cookies once you bake it.

Serving Size: 4

Cooking Time: 15 Minutes

Ingredients:

- ¾ cup butter
- 1 ¼ cups brown sugar
- 1 ½ teaspoons vanilla extract
- ¼ cup fresh milk
- A pinch of salt
- 1-½ cups toasted flour
- 5 tablespoons semisweet chocolate chips

Instructions:

1. Place butter in a pan then preheat over low heat until just foaming. The butter will smell nutty.

2. Remove the butter from the heat then let it cool.

3. Once the butter is cool, stir in salt, brown sugar, and vanilla extract then mix well.

4. Next, pour fresh milk over the mixture then add toasted flour to the mixture. Beat until becoming soft dough.

5. Add chocolate chips to the mixture then mix until just combined.

6. Freeze the cookie dough for an hour then remove from the freezer.

7. Take a scoop of cookie dough and drop in a cup.

8. Serve and enjoy immediately.

Cappuccino Coconut Cookie Dough Truffles

Coffee lovers will absolutely love this recipe. Everyone else will also enjoy it. The truffles have an authentic cappuccino flavor with a mild coconut taste in every ball. It is perfect for an evening talk with tea or coffee.

Serving Size: 4

Cooking Time: 1 Hour 10 Minutes

Ingredients:

- ¾ cup butter
- ½ cup powdered sugar
- 1 pasteurized egg
- ¾ cup toasted coconut flour
- 2 tablespoons non-dairy creamer
- 2 tablespoons cocoa powder
- 1-tablespoon instant coffee
- ¼ teaspoon cinnamon
- ¼ cup mini chocolate chips
- 1 cup chopped dark chocolate

Instructions:

1. Combine the dry ingredients—toasted coconut flour, non-dairy creamer, cocoa powder, instant coffee, and cinnamon in a bowl. Stir until combined then set aside.

2. Place butter and powdered sugar in a mixing bowl then using a mixer beat until smooth and creamy.

3. Add pasteurized egg to the mixture then beat again until fluffy. Remove the mixer.

4. Add the dry mixture to the mixture then using a wooden or rubber spatula mix until becoming soft dough.

5. Shape the cookie dough into small balls forms and fill each ball with mini chocolate chips.

6. Arrange the cookie dough balls in a baking tray then freeze for 15 minutes until cold and firm.

7. In the meantime, melt the chopped dark chocolate then let it warm.

8. After 15 minutes in the freezer, remove the cookie dough balls from the freezer and dip each cookie dough ball in the melted chocolate.

9. Arrange the coated cookie dough truffles on a baking tray and refrigerate for 15 minutes.

10. Remove the cookie dough truffles from the refrigerator and serve.

11. Enjoy cold.

Cinnamon Cookie Dough with Date Sugar

It is a bit unbelievable that something so sweet yet healthy exists. This cookie dough uses date sugar that is well known as healthy sugar. It makes this raw dough is completely safe to be eaten even by people with diabetes, of course, in a limited amount. If you like herbs, besides cinnamon, you can also add nutmeg and a pinch of ground clove. It will enrich not only the taste but also the aroma.

Serving Size: 4

Cooking Time: 20 Minutes

Ingredients:

- 2 teaspoons cinnamon
- ¼ cup palm sugar
- 1-cup butter
- 1-¼ cups date sugar
- 1 ½ teaspoons vanilla
- ¼ teaspoon salt
- 1-¾ cups toasted flour

Instructions:

1. Combine palm sugar with a teaspoon of cinnamon in a bowl then stir well. Set aside.

2. Using a mixer beat butter until soft then add date sugar and vanilla to the butter. Beat again until creamy.

3. Next, stir in salt and toasted flour to the mixture then using a wooden or rubber spatula mix until becoming dough.

4. Shape the dough into small balls forms and roll each ball in the cinnamon and palm sugar mixture. Make sure that each cookie dough ball is completely coated with sugar and cinnamon mixture.

5. Once it is done, arrange the cookie dough on a serving dish.

6. Serve and enjoy.

Gingery Cookie Dough with Sesame Seeds

With a perfect measurement of ingredients and seasoning, this recipe serves yummiest ginger cookie dough that you have ever tasted before. Dates are used in this recipe to give natural sweetness. However, if you have difficulty finding dates due to the changing seasons, you may change it with coconut sugar or brown sugar using the same measurement.

Serving Size: 4

Cooking Time: 20 Minutes

Ingredients:

- ¾ cup pitted dates
- ¾ cup toasted flour
- 1 ½ teaspoons ginger powder
- ¾ teaspoon cinnamon
- ¾ teaspoon vanilla
- 2 tablespoons olive oil
- 1-cup sesame seeds

Instructions:

1. Combine toasted flour with ginger powder and cinnamon then stir well.

2. Place pitted dates in a food processor then process until smooth.

3. Transfer the pitted dates to a mixing bowl then mix with the dry mixture until becoming dough.

4. Pour olive oil and vanilla over the dough and mix until soft.

5. Shape the cookie dough into small balls forms and roll each ball into the sesame seeds.

6. Arrange the cookie dough balls on a serving dish then serve.

7. Enjoy right away.

Green Tea Cookie Dough with Garbanzo Beans

It cannot be denied that garbanzo beans are a superfood. Because of the rich content of vitamin, protein, mineral, and dietary fiber, garbanzo beans are now famous as beneficial legumes. Now, it becomes a favorite for those who want to live a healthier lifestyle. This cookie dough combines garbanzo beans with green tea. Surely, that combination results in very scrumptious cookie dough. However, if you want other flavors, you can add or substitute green tea with other flavors, it's up to you. Besides that, you can also add any kinds of topping on tops, such as chopped roasted almonds, chocolate chips, sprinkles, and many other toppings.

Serving Size: 4

Cooking Time: 20 Minutes

Ingredients:

- ¾ cup cooked garbanzo beans
- ¼ cup almond milk
- 3 tablespoons butter
- ¼ cup coconut sugar
- 1 cup toasted almond flour
- ½ cup vanilla protein powder
- 1-tablespoon green tea powder

Instructions:

1. Place cooked garbanzo beans in a food processor then process until smooth.

2. Add the remaining ingredients—almond milk, butter, coconut sugar, toasted almond flour, vanilla protein powder, and green tea powder to the food processor then process until becoming soft dough.

3. Transfer the cookie dough to a container then cover with plastic wrap.

4. Refrigerate the cookie dough for at least an hour or until cold and firm.

5. Scoop the cookie dough and drop on serving cups.

6. Serve and enjoy.

Palm Sugar Cookie Dough with Traditional Herbs

If you are looking for unique and special cookie dough, then this one is an answer. Mainly made from cashews that are absolutely delicious and seasoned with traditional herbs, this cookie dough is a great choice to serve. One tip to make the appearance of the dough balls appealing to the eye, you must sift the palm sugar before using it to evenly coat the cookie dough balls.

Serving Size: 4

Cooking Time: 40 Minutes

Ingredients:

- 2 cups roasted cashews
- 1 cup pitted dates
- ¾ tablespoon cinnamon
- 1-teaspoon ginger
- ½ teaspoon nutmeg
- ¼ teaspoon salt
- 2 tablespoons milk
- ½ cup palm sugar

Instructions:

1. Place roasted cashews and pitted dates in a food processor then season with cinnamon, ginger, nutmeg, and salt.

2. Pour milk into the food processor then process the entire ingredients until becoming soft dough.

3. Cover the soft dough with plastic wrap then refrigerate for 20 minutes.

4. After 20 minutes in the refrigerator, remove the cookie dough and shape into small balls forms.

5. Roll each cookie dough ball in the coconut sugar then arrange on a serving dish.

6. Serve and enjoy.

Coconut Flaxseeds Cookie Dough Bites

There is no doubt that coconut gives us lots of benefits. Coconut sugar is known as one of the healthiest sugars as well as coconut butter and coconut flour. This cookie dough is not only safe but also healthy. To enhance the coconut taste and aroma, you can fry the coconut flakes without oil for a minute or two before using.

Serving Size: 4

Cooking Time: 40 Minutes

Ingredients:

- ¾ cup coconut butter
- ¼ cup coconut sugar
- 2 tablespoons maple syrup
- 1-teaspoon vanilla
- 1 cup toasted coconut flour
- 3 tablespoons ground flaxseeds
- ½ cup coconut flakes

Instructions:

1. Place coconut butter and coconut sugar in a mixing bowl then using a hand mixer beat until creamy.

2. Pour maple syrup and vanilla to the mixture then beat again until fluffy. Remove the mixer.

3. Add ground flaxseeds and toasted coconut flour to the mixture then using a rubber or wooden spatula mix until becoming soft dough.

4. Take a scoop of cookie dough then shape into a ball. Repeat with the remaining dough.

5. Roll each cookie dough ball in the coconut flakes then arrange on a baking tray.

6. Refrigerate the cookie dough balls for at least 30 minutes before serving.

7. Serve and enjoy.

Peppermint Cookie Dough with Chocolate Chips

The word "mint" often refers to "fresh." Using mint extract and fresh mint leaves, this cookie dough serves a refreshing sensation that you probably haven't tried before. The taste of this cookie dough is absolutely wonderful since mint and chocolate generate a perfect harmony. If milk chocolate chips are not available, you may substitute with chopped dark chocolate.

Serving Size: 4

Cooking Time: 50 Minutes

Ingredients:

- ¾ cup butter
- ¾ cup granulated sugar
- ¼ cup coconut sugar
- 3 tablespoons fresh milk
- 1-teaspoon mint extract
- 1-½ teaspoons chopped mint leaves
- ¼ teaspoon green food coloring
- 1-½ cups toasted flour
- ¾ cup mini chocolate chips

Instructions:

1. Place butter in a mixing bowl then add granulated sugar and coconut sugar to the bowl.

2. Using a mixer beat the butter and sugar until creamy then add green food coloring, mint extract, and fresh milk. Beat for a few seconds until incorporated then remove the mixer.

3. Next, stir in toasted flour and chopped mint leaves to the butter mixture then mix until becoming dough.

4. Add mini chocolate chips to the dough and mix well.

5. Wrap the dough with plastic wrap then refrigerate for approximately 15 minutes.

6. After 30 minutes, take the cookie dough out of the refrigerator then unwrap it.

7. Shape the cookie dough into small balls forms then arrange on a serving dish.

8. Serve and enjoy.

Conclusion

Having known all of the techniques of making safe and tasty cookie dough with various mixtures and additional ingredients, you now finally have a lot of options for preparing some desserts or breakfasts for you and your family.

Please remember that although this cookbook has presented various tips and techniques, all of them are safe to eat; eating too much of something will never be good. Therefore, use this book when you feel like treating yourself and your loved ones to something sweet.

Maintaining a healthy lifestyle is the greatest investment you make in yourself. Because of that reason, this book can satisfy your cravings if you wish to eat cookie dough without all the guilt of indulging in your sweet tooth. You don't need to worry about the health problems that may result after eating these recipes as we have already shown you what techniques can be done to avoid any unnecessary health issues.

Have a wonderful experience making your own cookie dough and simply serve it on your dining table.

Author's Afterthoughts

THANK YOU

Thanks ever so much to each of my cherished readers for investing the time to read this book!

I know you could have picked from many other books, but you chose this one. So, a big thanks for downloading this book and reading all the way to the end.

If you enjoyed this book or received value from it, I'd like to ask you for a favor. Please take a few minutes to post an honest and heartfelt review on Amazon.com. Your support does make a difference and helps to benefit other people.

Thanks for your Reviews!

Rachael Rayner

CPSIA information can be obtained
at www.ICGtesting.com
Printed in the USA
LVHW060626040322
712557LV00005BB/398

9 798655 545380